NEW MEXICO

Copyright © 1986 Raintree Publishers Inc.

All rights reserved. No part of this book may be reproduced
or utilized in any form or by any means, electronic or mechanical,
including photocopying, recording or by any information storage
and retrieval system, without permission in writing from the
Publisher. Inquiries should be addressed to Raintree Publishers Inc.
330 East Kilbourn Avenue, Milwaukee, Wisconsin 53202.

A Turner Educational Services, Inc. book. Based on the Portrait
of America television series created by R.E. (Ted) Turner.

Library of Congress Number: 85-10832

1234567890   908988878685

Library of Congress Cataloging in Publication Data

Thompson, Kathleen.
  New Mexico.

  (Portrait of America)
  "A Turner book."
  Summary: Discusses the history, economy, culture,
and future of New Mexico. Also includes a state
chronology, pertinent statistics, and maps.
  1. New Mexico—Juvenile literature. [1. New Mexico]
I. Title. II. Series: Thompson, Kathleen. Portrait of
America.
F796.3.T46 1985   978.9   85-10832
ISBN 0-86514-439-7 (lib. bdg.)
ISBN 0-86514-514-8 (softcover)

Cover Photo: New Mexico Tourism and Travel Division, Photo by Mark Nohl

★ ★ ★ ★ ★
Portrait of AMERICA

NEW MEXICO

Kathleen Thompson

Photographs from Portrait of America programs
courtesy of Turner Program Services, Inc.

A TURNER BOOK
RAINTREE PUBLISHERS

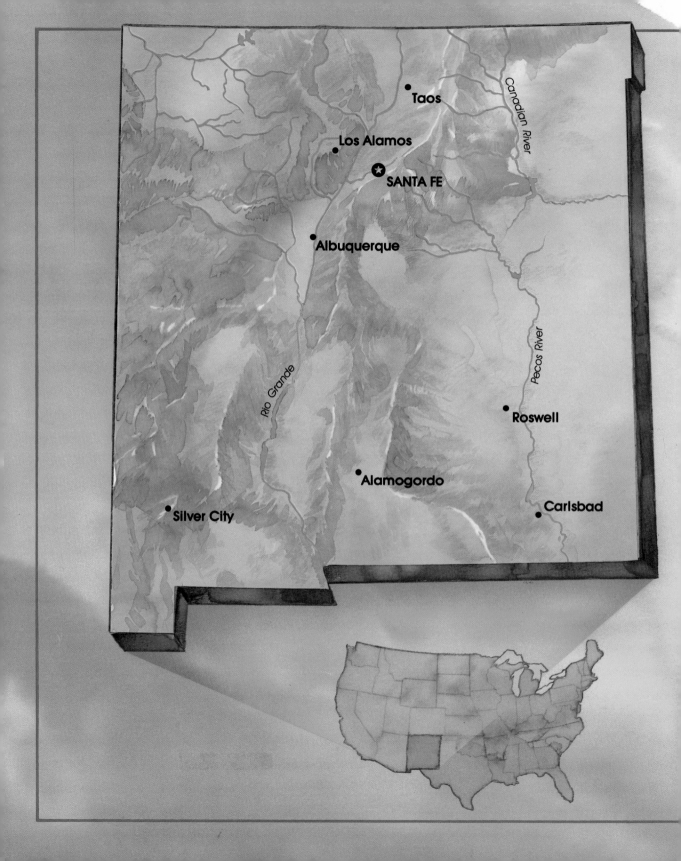

CONTENTS

Introduction   7

New Mexico, Land of Enchantment   10
   David Ortega, New Mexico Weaver   20

Working with What the Land Has to Give   24
   Acequias—Lifelines for the Land   32

Pueblos, Fiestas, and Rodeos   34
   The Atomic Split   38

New Versus Old in New Mexico   40
   Important Historical Events in New Mexico   44
   New Mexico Almanac   45
   Places to Visit/Annual Events   46
   Map of New Mexico Counties   47

Introduction

Twenty thousand years ago . . .

That's eighteen thousand years before Jesus was born in Nazareth. It's fifteen thousand years before the Great Pyramids of Egypt were built.

Twenty thousand years ago, there were Indians living on the land we call New Mexico.

Ten thousand years ago, there were Indian hunters using spears in northeastern New Mexico. We know because we've found their stone spearheads at Folsom.

At about the time of the great Greek and Roman civilizations in Europe, the Anasazi Indians were creating stone apartment houses of up to 800 rooms. They raised corn and cotton, and they tamed the wild turkeys that wandered the land.

The New Mexico desert, near Carrizozo.

8

In the cold of winter, they wore beautiful robes made of turkey feathers.

From this ancient tribe came the Pueblo Indians.

Later, about the time that Christopher Columbus first stepped onto American land, the Pueblos were joined by the Navajo and the Apache, the Utes and the Comanches. They all lived, hunted, and built their homes on the dry but beautiful land. They found ways to live with the land—ways that are still being used today in New Mexico.

The Carlos Vierra House, in Santa Fe (left), was built in 1918-1920. It was restored in 1980. Below is a small adobe house.

New Mexico, Land of Enchantment

"This is the place that I saw the daylight for the first time, right here in New Mexico. I've been to different places, but this is my motherland. You know, when the daylight comes up—no matter where I was—I remember about this land."

New Mexico: artists, writers, Navajos, and nuclear reactors.

"New Mexico is one of those subtle sorts of places, I think, which gradually affects the people who come here. People do not affect this place. This place affects people."

New Mexico is a beautiful place. The land and the sky are streaked with colors. Red, purple, blue, and the earth colors—the brown of the clay and dirt, the soft green of the grass.

A yucca plant, New Mexico's state flower.

It's a dramatic kind of beauty, with deep caverns and huge slabs of rock piling up toward the sky.

No matter what part of New Mexico you're talking about, you always seem to go back to the beauty and the land. There's the rich and ancient culture of the Indians. There's the rocket research. There's the colorful culture of the Spanish. And there are all the things that go to make up a modern, twentieth-century world.

But always, in the end, you come back to the land.

The first Europeans to come into New Mexico were the Spanish. It happened accidentally, in a way. There was a group of Spanish explorers looking for gold in Florida in 1528. Near the Texas coast, their ship was wrecked, and most of the men drowned. But Álvar Núñez Cabeza de Vaca and three others made it to the shore.

For eight years, they wandered the Southwest. Finally, they found their way to a Spanish settlement in Mexico. The

At the right are the Gila Cliff Dwellings. Now a historic monument, they were once the site of an Indian settlement.

New Mexico Tourism and Travel Division, Photo by Mark Nohl

people there told the explorers stories of seven fabulously rich cities, the seven cities of Cibola.

Of course, other Spanish explorers immediately set out to look for the seven cities. One of them, a priest named Marcos de Niza, asked one of Cabeza de Vaca's companions, Estevanico—also called Estéban—to be his guide. Together, they traveled into New Mexico and claimed it for Spain. When they went back to Mexico, Marcos de Niza said that he had seen one of the seven rich cities from a distance. That led other explorers to keep searching.

The explorers never found the golden cities of their dreams. But in 1598, a Spanish colony was created in New Mexico. Juan de Oñate put up the money for it and became governor of the Spanish province of New Mexico.

In 1610, Pedro de Peralta became governor and moved the capital to Santa Fe.

This Spanish colony was a poor one. About the only thing that kept it going was the Roman Catholic church. Missionary priests came from Spain to try to

Above is a painting of Diego de Vargas. He was the governor of New Mexico toward the close of the seventeenth century.

teach Christianity to the Indians. But the church didn't get along with the government. And the Spaniards didn't get along with the Indians. Or, rather, the Indians didn't get along with the Spaniards, and with good reason.

The Spanish had better weapons than the Indians. And they used them to force the Indians to work for them. They also tried to force the Indians to stop worshipping their gods. Finally, an Indian named Popé, from the San Juan Pueblo, led a revolt against the Spanish. More than 400 Spaniards were killed. The rest ran away to El Paso, in what is now Texas.

But in 1692, the Spanish were back. It took four years of fighting for Diego de Vargas to defeat the Pueblo Indians. But he did. The priests and the Spanish colonists came back. This time, the Indians and the Spaniards found a way to live side by side fairly peacefully.

And that's the way it was for about 125 years.

Then, two things happened. First, trappers and traders started coming into New Mexico from the United States. This made the Spanish government nervous. Once the trappers started hunting on the land and once the traders began to bring in goods for the settlers, the soldiers wouldn't be far behind. The United States had already taken over most of the North American continent south of Canada. The Spanish were afraid they would take over the one Spanish colony that was left.

So they forced the trappers and traders to leave. Or they put them in prison. But it wasn't soldiers from the United States that the Spanish had to worry about. In 1821, Mexico won its independence from Spain, and New Mexico became a Mexican province.

At the same time, William Becknell, an American trader, opened the Santa Fe Trail. Traders began to bring goods into New Mexico from Missouri.

For twenty-five years, Mexico ruled the area. At one point, the people of New Mexico rebelled against the Mexican government, but their victory lasted for only a month. At another point, Texas tried to take over New Mexico. Texas was an independent country then. But the Texans were defeated.

Then, in 1846, Mexico and the United States went to war. The war lasted for two years, and when it was over, the United States owned New Mexico.

In 1850, New Mexico was organized as a territory. A territory was a part of the United

States but was not officially a state. This new territory didn't have exactly the same borders that New Mexico has today. It included Arizona, for example, and parts of Colorado, Nevada, and Utah. And it didn't include the land south of the Gila River. That still belonged to Mexico, but the United States bought it in 1853.

New Mexico got the boundaries that it has now in 1863.

During the Civil War, the people of New Mexico once more saw their land being fought over. Confederate forces from Texas captured a large part of the area early in the war. In 1862, Union forces won it back.

Back in the East, in New York and Boston and Philadelphia, the United States was becoming a civilized place. Buildings were getting taller and trains were getting faster. But New Mexico was still the Wild West. There would be a lot more fighting and a lot more shooting.

There was Kit Carson, for example. He was a frontiersman, a famous scout. He led New Mexican settlers against the Mescalero Apache and the Navajo tribes. The Indians were forced off their lands and onto reservations.

At the left is a scene at the Billy the Kid Pageant in Lincoln. Above is an actual photograph of Billy the Kid, whose real name was William H. Bonney.

During the 1870s, another war broke out. This time it was between cattle ranchers and the people who wanted to use the land for other things. There were a lot of outlaws fighting in the range war, including Billy the Kid.

General Lew Wallace was appointed territorial governor in 1878. He ended the Lincoln County War, as it was called, by sending in soldiers.

And all this time, the Indians never stopped fighting for their land and their way of life.

It was in 1886, just fourteen years before the beginning of the twentieth century, that Geronimo finally surrendered.

In 1912, New Mexico became a state. By that time, the railroads had connected the territory to the rest of the country. Mining and cattle ranching were both big business. The new state had a population of 330,000. But the fighting wasn't quite over. In 1916, Pancho Villa and his Mexican bandits raided the state. He killed sixteen people in the town of Columbus and then fled back to Mexico. The United States Army followed him but didn't find him.

In the 1920s a drought hit New Mexico. Without rain, the crops died in the fields. Ranchers weren't able to feed their cattle.

At the right is an antenna that receives signals from spacecraft and artificial satellites. Above is an oil pump in one of New Mexico's many oil fields.

Portrait of America

A lot of people lost their land and their savings. But there were new possibilities on the horizon.

Oil was discovered. All across the state, wells were drilled in the sun-baked clay. Then another important mineral was discovered, potash. Money started coming back into New Mexico. And in 1930, the Carlsbad Caverns became a national park. So tourists began to come into the state.

In World War II, the 200th Coast Artillery was in the Philippine Islands. It was a regiment of New Mexican soldiers. Many of them were killed. Many of them spent three years in a Japanese prison camp. And then the war ended. The United States dropped two atom bombs on the Japanese cities of Hiroshima and Nagasaki. The bombs had been made in New Mexico, at Los Alamos.

After the war ended, the United States government built more and more research laboratories and testing locations in New Mexico. More money came into the state from the federal government for developing nuclear power and rockets. New Mexico's population grew as more workers came in to take government jobs.

In 1950, Paddy Martinez, a Navajo Indian, found uranium in New Mexico.

Today, New Mexico is an important center of space and nuclear research. Its mineral resources have become important to the whole country. And the tourist industry is growing.

The Spanish and Indian cultures remain a big part of life in New Mexico. But that life is very different from the land where the Anasazi raised wild turkeys and the explorers thought they had seen the seven cities of gold.

The Indians below are in the small town of Pojoaque, near Santa Fe. They are performing a ceremonial cloud dance.

New Mexico Tourism and Travel Division, Photo by Mark Nohl

David Ortega, New Mexico Weaver

"This blanket was made by my father. He was eighty-nine years old when he made this. He was a weaver for over seventy years."

Spanish settlers brought the art of weaving to Chimayo, New Mexico. The Ortega family has been weaving for seven generations. Today, David Ortega's company helps keep the community alive. Because of the weaving, people are able to make a living and preserve the traditions of the valley. That's very important in Chimayo.

"This particular valley is very self-sufficient because we have water and you can grow almost anything here. People who have any acreage at all can make a livelihood, and, well, people have their roots here—they just stick around. They don't sell the land. The people—the fathers and the mothers— hold their lands for their sons or their grandchildren. Even though they don't

At the left is David Ortega. Above is the inside of his weaving company.

21

live here, they expect them to get back someday."

David Ortega's weaving business is a cottage industry. That means that he supplies people with looms and material. Then the people work in their own homes. More than a hundred weavers work regularly for David Ortega.

For David, and for the others who live there, Chimayo is a very special place.

"This was the original settlement. And it was like a fort. They would enclose themselves in here and protect themselves from raids from the Indians, and they were safe. Chimayo is considered one of twelve villages in this country that is old, that has never grown, but it has never died."

Below are buildings from the original settlement in Chimayo.

New Mexico Tourism and Travel Division, Photo by Mark Nohl

Working with What the Land Has to Give

In New Mexico, everything begins and ends with the land.

On the east coast, factories and cities replaced a wooded wilderness. The rolling farmlands of the Midwest were once forests. And people came into these states and made what they wanted, often in spite of what the land offered them. Well, it just doesn't work that way in New Mexico.

The important difference is water. It takes water to run factories. It takes water to keep the amber waves of grain growing. In New Mexico, there is little water. What water there is must be saved and protected to make the land produce food.

But the land has other things to give. And the people of

A present-day irrigation canal.

25

New Mexico have worked with the land to make a rich and growing culture.

New Mexico is a big state. In terms of area, only Alaska, Texas, California, and Montana are bigger. But only about 1,300,000 people live in the entire state. That's about eleven people per square mile. And about 40 percent of those people live in the state's two big urban areas.

A lot of the land in New Mexico is covered with mountains, with canyons and rocky deserts. This beautiful scenery brings thousands of tourists into the state every year.

And the land is not just beautiful. It is rich.

For one thing, the land of New Mexico is rich in minerals, minerals that are important to the entire country. There are the energy minerals—coal, natural gas, petroleum and uranium. About one-third of New Mexico's mineral production is natural gas. Second in value is oil.

At the right an Indian woman is taking care of a flock of sheep. At the far right is Albuquerque.

The biggest part of New Mexico's agriculture is ranching. The ranchers above are moving a herd of cattle. The children at the right are feeding milk to the calves.

New Mexico is a big part of the Southwest's petroleum belt.

New Mexico produces more uranium than any other state. It's one of the world's leading sources of this important mineral. In fact, about half of this country's total output of uranium comes from New Mexico. And uranium is the main source of nuclear energy.

As this country and the world search for more and better sources of energy to support our modern lifestyles, New Mexico's energy minerals become more important and more valuable.

The dry, stony land of New Mexico gives up other minerals as well. The state is the leading producer of potash, a vital material for fertilizer. The green farmlands of the Midwest would not be quite so green if it were not for the potash that is mined in New Mexico.

There's copper here, and gypsum. Perlite, salt, sand and gravel, zinc, clay, gemstones—the list of minerals goes on and on. In all, 65 percent of all goods produced in New Mexico are minerals.

But mining, important as it is, remains only a part of the picture. About 21 percent of the

goods produced in New Mexico are agricultural. New Mexico has more than 11,000 farms and ranches.

Ranching is the biggest part of New Mexico's agriculture. There are more cattle and sheep in the state than there are people, one and a half times as many, in fact.

The ranches cover millions of acres of land that is too dry for farming.

New Mexico farmland produces cotton, hay, and wheat, chiefly. Other important crops include corn, grain sorghum, pecans, and onions. And there are also dairy farms.

29

Most of the land used for farming has to be irrigated. Many farmers still use the irrigation ditches created hundreds of years ago by the Spanish. These ditches have to be tended carefully and constantly to keep the water flowing into the fields. That is just part of what New Mexico farmers have learned to do for the land that feeds them.

There are more modern methods of irrigation, too, of course. New dams have provided more water. And deep wells have been dug to bring water out of the ground.

Manufacturing accounts for about 14 percent of the goods produced in New Mexico. Food processing is number one. Other manufactured goods include electrical machinery and equipment; lumber and wood products; printed material; stone, clay, and glass products; and petroleum and coal products.

All of that gives us a good picture of the goods that are produced in New Mexico. But there's another picture that we have to take a look at.

More people are employed by the federal government in New

Mexico than in mining, agriculture, and manufacturing combined. The federal government owns more than one-third of the land in the state. A lot of that is national forest, grasslands, and Indian reservations. The rest is primarily used for defense and nuclear research. About one-quarter of all the people who have jobs in New Mexico work for the government.

These government jobs, and much of New Mexico's industry, are part of the nuclear age. The first atomic bomb was made and exploded in New Mexico. The necessary uranium is here, and so are the huge open spaces, the miles of desert where no one lives. On this land, nuclear weapons have been tested. And sources of nuclear power that could solve many of our energy problems, but could also hold untold dangers, have been developed.

Here on the New Mexico land, the nuclear age lives side by side with stone-lined irrigation ditches built two hundred years ago.

At the far left is a portion of Santa Fe. Below is the Los Alamos Scientific Laboratory, where scientists study the uses of nuclear energy.

Los Alamos National Laboratory

Acequias—Lifelines for the Land

Without water, there is no life. In New Mexico, water comes to a part of the land through irrigation ditches that were built two hundred years ago. The people who live on this land still care for the ditches, the *acequias.*

"We want to live from the ground, from the earth. We consider the earth over here as our mother, and we must maintain it clean and preserve it clean. Our waters run in the ditches over here, which I love and everybody loves over here."

The people in the community have meetings to talk about the care of the ditches, to plan what needs to be done and who will do it. It takes a lot of people to keep these fragile streams of water clear, to keep the water running.

"When the ditches are dry, everybody in the community feels discouraged because they can't see the water running in the ditches. And every spring the majordomos and the commissions summon the people at a certain day or days to clean this ditch."

The Spanish people, the people who have lived here since the ditches were built, understand how important they are. But some of the newcomers don't understand.

"Each year new people come to town . . . and they buy property along the ditch. They become **parsiontes** *on the irrigation system, but they're not really interested. . . . Some of the people sell their water rights because, you know, you come into town and you need a bundle to — let's say — start building a house. You can get a lot of money for your irrigation rights. And so people do that. They retire the water on the ditch and then they're not interested in working on the acequia anymore."*

John Nichols (right) is a writer who lives in Taos. He is one of many who want to maintain the tradition of the ancient acequias (below).

It's hard for people who are used to today's technology to believe that it can be so important to clean up the rubbish from a stream of water that may not be two feet wide. It doesn't seem efficient. It doesn't seem modern. And yet, when the ditches are not tended, the land dies.

"People that used to live in the city— they're tired. I don't blame them. I wouldn't live in the city if you paid me. I don't blame them for coming over here. This is a beautiful country, but I think they should take care of the land—build their houses, yes, but not spoil it."

Courtesy of Museum of New Mexico, Photo by T. Harmon Parkhurst

Pueblos, Fiestas, and Rodeos

The culture of New Mexico is as richly colored as the landscape. For one thing, New Mexico's roots in other countries remain very close to the surface in modern America.

In many parts of the United States, our Native American heritage has been almost entirely lost or destroyed. This is not true in New Mexico. A glance at the Indian ceremonies and yearly rituals that still take place all over the state tells the story.

In late June, there is the Mescalero Apache Indian Celebration in Ruidoso. In July there is the Puyé Cliff Ceremonial at Santa Clara Pueblo. In August, there is the Green Corn Dance at Santa Domingo Pueblo. The list goes on and on.

Zozobra, a huge paper puppet, is burned at a festival in order to rid people of their troubles.

Everywhere, the art of the Indian is part of the style of New Mexico. The people cherish the beautifully woven rugs, the hammered metal jewelry, the masks and feather decorations. In fact, the way of life of an Indian in New Mexico today may be very much like the life lived by an ancestor two hundred years ago. Many still live in pueblos or on reservations.

But the traditions of the New Mexico Indian are always in danger from the modern world. An Indian farmer may have to fight to keep strip-miners away from the land. A hill that an Indian family treasures for the part it plays in their history and rituals may seem to an outsider simply a rich source of minerals.

Still, the Native American culture, even as it changes, remains a vital part of New Mexico life.

Along with the Indian ceremonials in New Mexico, you'll see the Spanish fiestas. There's the Feria Artesana in Albuquerque, the Fiesta de Santa Fe, the Christmas Eve Luminaria Tours in Albuquerque.

Churches built by the Spanish missionaries figure strongly in the architecture of New Mexico. Many communities still speak mostly Spanish, and the music of Spain and Mexico provides a background to much of New Mexico life.

These cultures are preserved in places like the Museum of International Folk Art in Santa Fe, and the Wheelwright Museum, also in Santa Fe, which has a large collection of Navajo ceremonial art.

Then there are the cowboys. Because of the huge grazing ranges in New Mexico, cattle ranchers came and brought with them still another part of the New Mexico cultural picture. Cowboy hats and boots are as familiar as woven blankets. Rodeos are as much a part of life as fiestas.

It's true that you'll find all of these cultural threads in any southwestern state. But New Mexico has a unique balance, in part because the population is unusually balanced. Most people who live in New Mexico are the children and grandchildren of people who were in one of the three major groups that settled the area—the Indians, the Span-

The annual Hot Air Balloon Festival in Albuquerque.

ish, and the English-speaking Americans.

And then there is another group that is important in New Mexico's culture. The beauty of New Mexico has drawn hundreds of artists and writers. These are people who could do their work anywhere but have chosen New Mexico.

The state has always attracted artists. Painters come for the landscape. Potters come for the clay. All of the artists come for the dramatic beauty of the land and the rich cultural mix. One of America's greatest artists, Georgia O'Keeffe, has lived and worked in New Mexico for many years, inspired by the stark and beautiful land.

Writers have come here, too. The English writer D.H. Lawrence and several of his friends came to New Mexico in the 1920s. They helped to create an artist's colony in the Taos area. Other writers followed.

And writers have written about New Mexico, too. Willa Cather set one of her finest books, *Death Comes for the Archbishop,* in New Mexico. Conrad Richter wrote *The Sea of Grass* about the struggle between ranchers and farmers in New Mexico. Mary Austin wrote beautiful English adaptations of Indian songs and poems.

New Mexico is a place where art and beauty seem to be very much at home.

An atom bomb blast . . . Tony Price . . . and one of his sculptures.

The Atomic Split

"Once the atomic bomb was detonated down at Trinity Site, down near Alamogordo, and once it was known to everybody in the world by the shots at Hiroshima and Nagasaki, [then] it was known across the entire scientific and technical world that there was no basic natural obstacle to making a nuclear explosion."

In the small town of Los Alamos, in 1943, hundreds of our country's best scientists came together. It was a very secret gathering. No one was supposed to know what was happening in this lonely town in the New Mexico desert.

And no one did know, until two atom bombs fell on Japan. That was the beginning of the nuclear age.

"I guess I was simply sure that the United States' monopoly on nuclear weapons would last only a few years. Actually, it lasted just a little more than two. Then the Russians got their bomb."

The people of New Mexico have mixed feelings about being the home of The Bomb. Many see it as necessary, a way to prevent war. They have made sacrifices because they believe it is their duty as Americans.

"Looks to me like what it boils down to is like President Kennedy said about what you can do for your country, not what your country does for you. We all have to make a contribution and a sacrifice."

Others in New Mexico feel differently. One artist, Tony Price, expresses those feelings in sculpture made from metal parts thrown away by Los Alamos.

"It was always kind of spooky, going up to Los Alamos, the birthplace of the nuclear age, to get these things. They always had a kind of spirit of death hanging over the parts. . . . Ten, twelve years later I began to have the feeling of the horror of this, and that maybe there would be a way to express with these parts a message about the horror of nuclear war."

New Versus Old
in New Mexico

"We're living right in the middle of a proposed mining area and also the proposed railroad right-of-way. My family is very religious, and my mother is the medicine woman, and we have a very big heart for our land, which is our Mother Earth. We have very much concern about what they are going to do."

Alice Ramon is a Navajo. She lives in Chaco Canyon, where the Anasazi Indians made their home long ago. Recently, a huge electric power plant was proposed. It would be built on the edge of the Canyon, not far from the ancient Anasazi ruins.

People like Frank Chee Willetto, a part of the Navajo tribal council, worry about the plant and the strip mining that is also being planned.

Chaco Canyon.

"It's going to be a tremendous change on the culture, which means about ten, twenty years from now, our culture is going to become practically completely ruined—because the people that move in are not going to be practicing the same culture. Very few people will respect the culture we have here."

As New Mexico comes more and more to depend on its mineral resources, this conflict of old and new will come up again and again. The riches buried in the land mean jobs and money. But there are other riches that are harder to see.

"If you look down there, that is a place where the family that lives there had a three-day ceremony, and during these three days a lot of traditional blessings—sacred blessings and also blessings of traditional objects—were made. A lot of sacred objects were made, and these sacred objects were put on the hill back down that way. To the family that lives there, that hill is considered a sacred site. This family would not dare even attempt to destroy that hill. It's just not our way. It's just not the Navajo way. It's not the Indian way."

The ancient ruins of the Anasazi may save Chaco Canyon. They are a valuable historical and archaeological site. The strip mining and the power plant might put them in danger.

But there will always be another hill, another place sacred to the people who live there, and another place where the riches of the land lie buried under the culture of the people.

New Mexico faces an exciting future. Its mineral resources could help solve energy problems for the entire country. At any rate, it is certain to be a big part of our plans and dreams for a better world.

Another thing in the future of New Mexico is water. The San Juan-Chama project brings water through tunnels from the San Juan River. Reservoirs near Chama and Santa Fe are providing those communities with water they've never had before. Finding more water and better ways to irrigate will bring more opportunities for farming and for industry.

Winter sports resorts are bringing in more tourists. Income from tourism grows every year.

In the past, the people of New Mexico have found ways of keeping the old ways alive. Now, they are faced with greater chal-

Leonard Tsosie (right) is a lawyer who is working to maintain New Mexico traditions at the same time that the state moves toward the future.

lenges than ever before. And, as always, the biggest problems and the greatest rewards will lie in living with the land.

Important Historical Events in New Mexico

1539 Marcos de Niza, a priest, explores New Mexico.

1540 Francisco Vásquez de Coronado begins a two-year exploration and conquest of New Mexico.

1598 Juan de Oñate founds the first permanent Spanish colony at San Juan, near the Chalma River.

1610 Pedro de Peralta, governor of the colony, moves the capital to Santa Fe.

1680 After years of a forced-labor system and religious suppression, Pueblo Indians revolt and drive the Spaniards out of New Mexico.

1692 Diego de Vargas, a Spanish governor, reconquers New Mexico.

1821 Mexico wins its independence from Spain and makes New Mexico a Mexican province. Captain William Becknell opens the Santa Fe Trail, a trade route between New Mexico and Missouri.

1846 The U.S. declares war on Mexico. U.S. General Stephen W. Kearny takes over New Mexico.

1848 The Mexican War ends, and Mexico gives New Mexico to the United States.

1850 The U.S. Congress creates the Territory of New Mexico.

1853 The Gadsden Purchase adds the Gila River area to New Mexico.

1864 Colonel Kit Carson defeats the Navajo and Mescalero Apache Indians, who are forced to live on reservations.

1876 Ranchers and other groups battle for control of Lincoln County in what was called the Lincoln County War.

1886 Geronimo surrenders to the U.S. Army in Arizona, thus ending the Apache Wars.

1912 New Mexico becomes the 47th state on January 6. The capital is Santa Fe.

1916 Elephant Butte Dam, on the Rio Grande River, is completed.

1922 Large oil fields are discovered in San Juan County.

1930 Carlsbad Caverns National Park is created.

1945 The first atomic bomb is exploded at Trinity Site, near Alamogordo, on July 16.

1949 Los Alamos becomes the 32nd county.

1962 The Navajo Dam on the San Juan River is completed.

New Mexico Almanac

Nickname. The Land of Enchantment.

Capital. Santa Fe.

State Bird. Roadrunner.

State Flower. Yucca.

State Tree. Piñon.

State Motto. *Crescit Eundo* (It grows as it grows.)

State Song. O, Fair New Mexico.

State Abbreviations. N. Mex. or N.M. (traditional); NM (postal).

Statehood. January 6, 1912, the 47th state.

Government. Congress: U.S. senators, 2; U.S. representatives, 3. **State Legislature:** senators, 42; representatives, 70. **Counties:** 32.

Area. 121,666 sq. mi. (315,113 sq. km), 5th in size among the states.

Greatest Distances. north/south, 391 mi. (629 km); east/west, 352 mi. (566 km.).

Elevation. Highest: Wheeler Peak, 13, 161 ft. (4,011 m); **Lowest:** Red Bluff Reservoir, 2,817 ft. (859 m).

Population. 1980 Census: 1,299,968 (28% increase over 1970), 37th among the states. **Density:** 11 persons per sq. mi. (4 persons per sq. km.). **Distribution:** 69% urban, 31% rural. **1970 Census:** 1,017,055.

Economy. Agriculture: beef cattle, cotton, milk, hay. **Manufacturing:** food products, electric and electronic equipment, printed materials, lumber and wood products. **Mining:** natural gas, petroleum, natural gas liquids, uranium, copper, potassium salts.

Places to Visit

Carlsbad Caverns National Park
Chaco Canyon.
Gila Wilderness.
Gila Cliff Dwellings.
Los Alamos Bradbury Science Hall
  and Museum.
Puyé Cliff Dwellings.
San Miguel Mission.
White Sands National Monument.

Annual Events

Dances, at most Indian pueblos (Easter).
Green Corn Dance at San Felipe Pueblo (May 1).
Apache Indian Ceremonial in Mescalero (July 4).
"Billy the Kid" Pageant in Lincoln (early August).
New Mexico State Fair in Albuquerque (mid-September).
Taos Festival of the Arts (early October).
Navajo Fair in Shiprock (early October).
International Hot-Air Balloon Fiesta in Albuquerque (mid-October).

New Mexico Counties

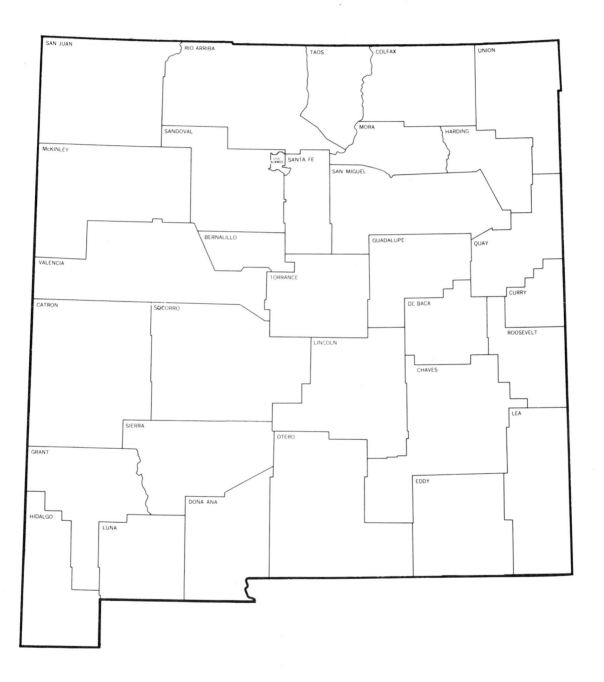